Cycle Clips

or,
Saddle Saws

OLEANDER

The Oleander Press
16 Orchard Street
Cambridge
CB1 1JT

www.oleanderpress.com

ISBN: 9781909349834

Printed in England

Cycle Clips

or,
Saddle Saws

Cycle Clips or, Saddle Saws

When I was a kid I used to pray every night for a new bicycle. Then I realised that the Lord doesn't work that way so I stole one and asked Him to forgive me.

~ Emo Philips

A woman without a man is like a fish without a bicycle.

~ Irina Dunn

Cycle Clips or, Saddle Saws

Every time I see an adult on a bicycle, I no longer despair for the future of the human race.

~ H. G. Wells

Communication is a skill that you can learn. It's like riding a bicycle or typing. If you're willing to work at it, you can rapidly improve the quality of every part of your life.

~ **Brian Tracy**

Newspapers are unable, seemingly, to discriminate between a bicycle accident and the collapse of civilization.

~ **George Bernard Shaw**

Cycle Clips or, Saddle Saws

Cycle tracks will abound in Utopia.
~ H.G. Wells

Cycle Clips or, Saddle Saws

Let a man find himself, in distinction from others, on top of two wheels with a chain – at least in a poor country like Russia – and his vanity begins to swell out like his tires.

~ Leon Trotsky

When man invented the bicycle he reached the peak of his attainments. Here was a machine of precision and balance for the convenience of man. And (unlike subsequent inventions for man's convenience) the more he used it, the fitter his body became. Here, for once, was a product of man's brain that was entirely beneficial to those who used it, and of no harm or irritation to others. Progress should have stopped when man invented the bicycle.

~ Elizabeth West

The bicycle has done more for the emancipation of women than anything else in the world.

~ **Susan B. Anthony**

I finally concluded that all failure was from a wobbling will rather than a wobbling wheel.

~ Frances E. Willard

Cycle Clips or, Saddle Saws

I want to ride my bicycle
I want to ride my bike
I want to ride my bicycle
I want to ride it where I like

~ Queen

You never have the wind with you – either it is against you or you're having a good day.

~ Daniel Behrman

On my tenth birthday, a bicycle and an atlas coincided as presents and a few days later I decided to cycle to India.

~ **Dervla Murphy**

Cycle Clips or, Saddle Saws

Cycling can be lonely, but in a good way.
~ **David Byrne**

Riding bicycles will not only benefit the individual doing it, but the world at large."
~ **Udo E. Simonis**

Truly, the bicycle is the most influential piece of product design ever."

~ Hugh Pearman

Cycling has encountered more enemies than any other form of exercise."
~ Louis Baudry de Saunier

Cycling is possibly the greatest and most pleasurable form of transport ever invented. It's like walking only with one-tenth of the effort. Ride through a city and you can understand its geography in a way that no motorist, contained by one-way signs and traffic jams, will ever be able to. You can whiz from one side to the other in minutes. You can overtake £250,000 sports cars that are going nowhere fast. You can park pretty much anywhere. It truly is one of the greatest feelings of freedom one can have in a metropolitan environment. It's amazing you can feel this free in a modern city."

~ Daniel Pemberton

Toleration is the greatest gift of the mind; it requires the same effort of the brain that it takes to balance oneself on a bicycle.

~ Helen Keller

Life is like a ten-speed bicycle. Most of us
have gears we never use.
~ Charles M. Schulz

Marriage is a wonderful invention; then again, so is a bicycle repair kit.

~ Billy Connolly

Guys would sleep with a bicycle if it had the right colour lip gloss on. They have no shame. They're like bull elks in a field.

~ Tori Amos

I'm lazy. But it's the lazy people who invented the wheel and the bicycle because they didn't like walking or carrying things.
~ **Lech Walesa**

Cycle Clips or, Saddle Saws

A few years ago, I bought an old red bicycle with the words *Free Spirit* written across its side - which is exactly what I felt like when I rode it down the street in a tie-dyed dress.

~ Drew Barrymore

Cycle Clips or, Saddle Saws

If I can bicycle, I bicycle.
~ David Attenborough

I used to bicycle to work across the George Washington Bridge, but my wife told me it wasn't professional.

~ Mehmet Oz

Cycle Clips or, Saddle Saws

The bicycle, the bicycle surely, should always be the vehicle of novelists and poets.
~ Christopher Morley

Because, you know, I can't work a bicycle pump.

~ Judi Dench

Riding a bicycle is about getting back to basics. It's good for the waistline and it's good for the wallet, is what I'm saying.

~ Phil Keoghan

I simply haven't the nerve to imagine a being, a force, a cause which keeps the planets revolving in their orbits and then suddenly stops in order to give me a bicycle with three speeds.

~ Quentin Crisp

Cycle Clips or, Saddle Saws

Well, I don't ever get excited. I haven't been excited since I got a Chopper bicycle when I was about 12. Once you get older you realise there's always a catch to everything.

~ Jack Dee

The city needs a car like a fish needs a bicycle.

~ Dean Kamen

But 17 years ago, I arrived at CNN with a suitcase, with my bicycle, and with about 100 dollars.

~ **Christiane Amanpour**

One of the most important days of my life was when I learned to ride a bicycle.
~ Michael Palin

My main form of transportation at that time was a bicycle, because bicycles could move though the crowd.

~ John Pomfret

The bicycle is a former child's toy that has now been elevated to icon status because, presumably, it can move the human form from pillar to post without damage to the environment.

~ Brock Yates

A bicycle has transformed my experience of London.

~ Iain Glen

Tens of thousands who could never afford to own, feed and stable a horse, had by this bright invention enjoyed the swiftness of motion which is perhaps the most fascinating feature of material life.

~ **Frances Willard**

Cycle Clips or, Saddle Saws

Socialism can only arrive by bicycle.
~ Jose Antonio Viera Gallo

The journey of life is like a man riding a bicycle. We know he got on the bicycle and started to move. We know that at some point he will stop and get off. We know that if he stops moving and does not get off he will fall off.

~ William Golding

In the 9th grade I began my first waged work for the West Side Drug store delivering prescriptions and sundries on my bicycle to customers who called in orders.

~ Vernon L. Smith

Life is like riding a bicycle: you don't fall off unless you stop pedalling.

~ Claude Pepper

Those who wish to control their own lives
and move beyond existence as mere clients
and consumers - those people ride a bike.
~ Wolfgang Sachs

There's a certain amount of freedom involved in cycling: you're self-propelled and decide exactly where to go. If you see something that catches your eye to the left, you can veer off there, which isn't so easy in a car, and you can't cover as much ground walking.

~ David Byrne

Cycle Clips or, Saddle Saws

My chosen exercise is cycling. I just love it.
~ Eric Bana

I've had so many experiences in cycling, but in some ways I have nothing left to prove. I have achieved more than I could have dreamed of, I've raced a lot longer than I thought I would. I know I can still be better, but I just don't know if I love it enough any more.

~ Clara Hughes

A friend of mine - a cameraman at MTV - lost a lot of weight from cycling, and I thought I'd try it, too, thinking whenever you look at a cyclist they all look super-skinny, so hey, why not? But then it turned into such a psychologically satisfying thing.

~ **Carson Daly**

Cycle Clips or, Saddle Saws

I think cycling has always had a tradition of
being a bit dapper, especially back in the
day.

~ David Millar

I think racing and riding are two different elements of cycling. You either want to or not depending on what you want to get out of it.

~ **Mark-Paul Gosselaar**

I have always struggled to achieve excellence. One thing that cycling has taught me is that if you can achieve something without a struggle it's not going to be satisfying.

~ Greg LeMond

I've just been reading about cycling. Yeah, I'm not that great at it but I like the challenge of it.

~ Joey Santiago

Cycling keeps me lean and I need to stay in shape, especially as I still like eating chocolate and ice-cream! I like to go mountain biking too.

~ Mark Webber

I love England though; I've been back a few times and just love it. My favourite thing to do there is going to museums and all the castles. Oh, and my husband and I went mountain biking across England on our honeymoon!

~ Catherine Bell

I used a bike in London and that's it. I learnt a lot about biking, and really got into it. Now I cycle regularly.

~ Jonny Lee Miller

I started mountain-bike riding two years ago, which is much better than riding a stationary bike in the gym. Mountain biking is a total body workout.

~ Samantha Stosur

My culinary wardrobe is the same as my biking wardrobe, just no shoes.

~ Lela Rose

Cycle Clips or, Saddle Saws

I guess I am basically most comfortable when I'm alone. As a kid, I was very much a loner. I love long distance running and long distance biking. A director once pointed out that those are all very isolated exercises you do for hours at a time.

~ Kevin Conroy

An intellectual is a man who doesn't know how to park a bike.

~ Spiro T. Agnew

If you worried about falling off the bike, you'd never get on.

~ Lance Armstrong

A lot of fun stuff happens when you go out on a bike compared to when you're in a car. You're more in the environment. It's enjoyable. Even when it's raining it's still fun.

~ **Stone Gossard**

Cycle Clips or, Saddle Saws

I'm no Lance Armstrong, but I do use a bike to get from place to place in Manhattan, a little bit of Brooklyn.

~ David Byrne

When I was a kid, I would do stupid things on my bike. I'd jump any ramp, I'd jump over people, I'd jump over things - always crashing, never hurting myself badly but always wanting to take physical risks.

~ **Eric Bana**

Cycle Clips or, Saddle Saws

I was hit by a car once on my bike, but I still rode home.

~ Amy Winehouse

Exercise is really important to me - it's therapeutic. So if I'm ever feeling tense or stressed or like I'm about to have a meltdown, I'll put on my iPod and head to the gym or out on a bike ride along Lake Michigan with the girls.

~ Michelle Obama

I've got the best of all worlds. It's every actor's dream to wake up in New York City and go to an acting job rather than to a restaurant to wash dirty dishes. And I live so close to the studios that I ride my bike to work.

~ **Christopher Meloni**

It was a weird mix of emotions. One day, your best friend could be killed. The day before, you could be celebrating him getting a brand-new bike.

~ **Jay-Z**

I remember riding my bike down the boardwalk with nowhere to go and looking at the girls. It was really innocent.

~ Mark Ruffalo

I look at being a capitalist businessperson like riding a bike - if I go too slowly, I'll fall over. Or it's kind of like a shark: if I stop swimming, I'll just die.

~ Andrew Mason

Cycle Clips or, Saddle Saws

The main thing I'm into is going about on a bike, taking random routes; I'm really into the idea of making up journeys, and just seeing where they take you, because they always end up taking you someplace freaky.
~ **Tom Jenkinson**

My dad gave me my first bike at 16. I soon fell off and was in a wheelchair for weeks. I haven't fallen since.

~ Hugh Laurie

Portland, Oregon won't build a mile of road without a mile of bike path. You can commute there, even with that weather, all the time.

~ **Lance Armstrong**

Cycling is based so much on form, on aesthetics, on class - the way you carry yourself on the bike, the sort of technique you have.

~ David Millar

Later, in the early teens, I used to ride my bike every Saturday morning to the nearest airport, ten miles away, push airplanes in and out of the hangars, and clean up the hangars.

~ **Alan Shepard**

I had a friend whose family had dinner together. The mother would tuck you in at night and make breakfast in the morning. They even had a spare bike for a friend. It just seemed so amazing to me.

~ Moon Unit Zappa

Cycle Clips or, Saddle Saws

I spent a couple of months just riding a bike doing my own training in the streets.
~ **Jonny Lee Miller**

Cycle Clips or, Saddle Saws

The first time I rode a bike I was four or five. I crashed into the back of a car.
~ **David Millar**

Cycle Clips or, Saddle Saws

Well, you go to Holland and everybody's on
a bike - nobody would think to have a car.
~ Stone Gossard

I've seen neighborhoods that I would have never driven though because I'm riding my bike, because I'm looking for side roads, looking for maybe more hills or less hills depending if I'm exercising or not. You see a lot more, and you get the flow of a city a lot more.

~ Stone Gossard

I believe there are two periods in life, one for the bike, the other for becoming active on one's work.

~ **Bernard Hinault**

For 20 years I've had the privilege of representing Canada around the globe... first on the bike and then on my blades. The experiences have shaped me into who I am today.

~ Clara Hughes

Perhaps people, and kids especially, are spoiled today, because all the kids today have cars, it seems. When I was young you were lucky to have a bike.

~ **James Cagney**

Cycle Clips or, Saddle Saws

I bike around New York City as a way of getting everywhere I need to go.

~ Lela Rose

Cycle Clips or, Saddle Saws

He didn't riot. He got on his bike and looked for work.

~ Norman Tebbit

The bicycle is a curious vehicle.   Its
passenger is its engine.

~ John Howard

Cycle Clips or, Saddle Saws

It never gets easier. You just go faster.
~ **Greg LeMond**

Until mountain biking came along, the bike scene was ruled by a small elite cadre of people who seemed allergic to enthusiasm.
~ Jacquie Phelan

Get a bicycle. You will not regret it if you live.

~ Mark Twain

Life is like riding a bicycle – in order to keep your balance, you must keep moving.

~ Albert Einstein

It is by riding a bicycle that you learn the contours of a country best, since you have to sweat up the hills and coast down them. Thus you remember them as they actually are, while in a motor car only a high hill impresses you, and you have no such accurate remembrance of country you have driven through as you gain by riding a bicycle.

~ **Ernest Hemingway**

The sound of a car door opening in front of you is similar to the sound of a gun being cocked.

~ Amy Webster

Cycle Clips or, Saddle Saws

The secret to mountain biking is pretty simple. The slower you go the more likely it is you'll crash.

~ Julie Furtado

The thing I like to do is not think of it as 'pain', but as 'that feeling I get when I'm riding correctly'. Do that long enough and you'll actually start to believe it.

~ Mark Hickey

Cycle Clips or, Saddle Saws

Nothing compares to the simple pleasure of a bike ride.

~ John F. Kennedy,

Cycle Clips or, Saddle Saws

It's not about the bike.
~ **Lance Armstrong**

Cycle Clips or, Saddle Saws

I thought of that while riding my bicycle.
~ **Albert Einstein**
(on the Theory of Relativity)

It is the unknown around the corner that turns my wheels.

~ Heinz Stucke,

Melancholy is incompatible with bicycling.
~ **James E. Starrs**

The bicycle is just as good company as most husbands and, when it gets old and shabby, a woman can dispose of it and get a new one without shocking the entire community.

~ Ann Strong

Think of bicycles as rideable art that can just about save the world.

~ **Grant Petersen**

Cycle Clips or, Saddle Saws

Don't buy upgrades, ride up grades.
~ **Eddy Merckx**

Cycle Clips or, Saddle Saws

As long as I breathe, I attack.
~ **Bernard Hinault**

The bicycle is the noblest invention of mankind.

~ William Saroyan

Whoever invented the bicycle deserves the thanks of humanity.
~ **Lord Charles Beresford**

Enough of this Sunday stroll. Let's hurt a little.

~ Muzzin, American Flyers

When the spirits are low, when the day appears dark, when work becomes monotonous, when hope hardly seems worth having, just mount a bicycle and go out for a spin down the road, without thought on anything but the ride you are taking.

~ **Arthur Conan Doyle**

Truth hurts. Maybe not as much as jumping on a bicycle with a seat missing, but it hurts.

~ Leslie Nielsen

Cycle Clips or, Saddle Saws

Bicycles are almost as good as guitars for meeting girls.

~ Bob Weir (Grateful Dead)

Cycling is the most popular sport because you don't have to pay for the ticket.
~ Pier Paolo Pasolini

Cycle Clips or, Saddle Saws

Bicycling is a healthy and manly pursuit with much to recommend it, and, unlike other foolish crazes, it has not died out.
~ The Daily Telegraph, 1877.

Cycle Clips or, Saddle Saws

I've got a bike,
You can ride it if you like.
It's got a basket,
A bell that rings
And things to make it look good.
I'd give it to you if I could
But I borrowed it.

~ Syd Barrett
(Pink Floyd)

Cycle Clips or, Saddle Saws

I began to feel that myself plus the bicycle equalled myself plus the world, upon whose spinning wheel we must all learn to ride, or fall into the sluice-ways of oblivion and despair. That which made me succeed with the bicycle was precisely what had gained me a measure of success in life — it was the hardihood of spirit that led me to begin, the persistence of will that held me to my task, and the patience that was willing to begin again when the last stroke had failed. And so I found high moral uses in the bicycle and can commend it as a teacher without pulpit or creed. She who succeeds in gaining the mastery of the bicycle will gain the mastery of life.

~ **Frances E. Willard**

No hour of life is lost that is spent in the saddle.

~ **Winston Churchill**

Cycle Clips or, Saddle Saws

Ride lots.
~ **Eddy Merckx**

Cycle Clips or, Saddle Saws

Thank you for choosing this book; we hope you enjoyed it.

Why not try the Cult Classic ~
The Night Climbers of Cambridge
by Whipplesnaith

available at all book retailers or from

www.oleanderpress.com

where the coupon
SADDLE13
gives 15% discount on any purchase.

Cycle Clips or, Saddle Saws

Why not keep up to date with special offers
from Oleander by liking us:
facebook.com/oleanderpress

or following us:
twitter.com/oleanderman

and you can win monthly prizes by signing
up for our infrequent, non-spammy
newsletter at:
oleanderpress.com

Printed in Poland
by Amazon Fulfillment
Poland Sp. z o.o., Wrocław